MW01482534

in ever friendship.
Love,
Shawna

Blue Feast

SHAWNA LEMAY

Shawna Lemay

NEWEST
PRESS

Library and Archives Canada Cataloguing in Publication
Lemay, Shawna, 1966-
Blue feast / Shawna Lemay.

Poems.
ISBN 1-896300-94-4

I. Title.

PS8573.E5358B58 2005   C811'.54   C2005-903531-5

Editor for the press: Douglas Barbour
Cover and interior design: Ruth Linka
Cover image: "Blue Poppy," oil on canvas, 2005, 10 x 10, by Robert Lemay
Author photo: Robert Lemay

NeWest Press acknowledges the support of the Canada Council for the Arts and the Alberta Foundation for the Arts, and the Edmonton Arts Council for our publishing program. We also acknowledge the financial support of the Government of Canada through the Book Publishing Industry Development Program (BPIDP) for our publishing activities.

NeWest Press
201–8540–109 Street
Edmonton, Alberta T6G 1E6
(780) 432-9427
www.newestpress.com

NeWest Press is committed to protecting the environment and to the responsible use of natural resources. This book is printed on 100% post-consumer recycled and ancient-forest-friendly paper. For more information please visit www.oldgrowthfree.com.

1   2   3   4   5   08   07   06   05

PRINTED AND BOUND IN CANADA

For Rob, soul-mate and true heart
and
For Chloe, my best thing

※ ※ ※

These poems were written toward the core of sadness as a way
of navigating the multiple registers that we dwell in at all times.
The reader who wants these poems is the reader who under-
stands the complicated joy that is entwined with sadness.

❋ ❋ ❋

A test of what is real is that it is hard and rough. Joys are found
in it, not pleasure. What is pleasant belongs to dreams.

—Simone Weil

But now I feel like saying things that comfort me and that are
somewhat free.

—Clarice Lispector

. . . for we are all poised on the brink of disaster, and at the same
time on the brink of unimaginable happiness, and yet somehow in
this dragonless age, we have learnt to balance, for the most part on
that narrow ridge that separates extreme joy from extreme sorrow,
to suspend ourselves endlessly at this counterpoint. . . .

—Sunetra Gupta

Table of Contents

� ✗ ✗

The Clearing

✗ ✗ ✗

Daring Instruction

※ ※ ※

A Kind of Gray Dream
❇ ❇ ❇

A Kind of Gray Dream

There is no artist without castoff feathers.
　　　　　　　—Helene Cixous

O, O, O. And where am I now?
At the yes, or, the no? or
what limbo?
To refuse barrenness and embrace dust.

It's time.

To comb my hair those hundred strokes.
To pin the antique brooch to my heart.
It's time to take it all off
disrobe slough peel.

It's time to write letters of praise
slide them into the capacious handbag
and stroll to the postbox.

I want this to be everything
should be calling to nothing.
Did you think these were poems?
Ink?

The truth is I never feel equal to the imperative task
throwing the feather boa over and around and back.
Tossing the bottle into the sea.

And it's sing and dance and sashay, shhhh
and it's quiet now
and easy does it
into the gate and into the bird cage
leave the jewels on the chest

and back out again
fasten the hasp and
disappear.

Meanwhile back at the chaise longue
now I must learn to become invisible
and in this way wait for the message.
Who would pass it to one who is not sheer? crystal?

The guilt of this easy hunger. . . .

And I draw the loose feathers
around my nakedness
the feathers that stack themselves
around the lion claw feet
like rose petals
in sticky pyramids like petit-fours.

The feathers
am I sure they are feathers?
arrive deliberately unbidden
and to cast them off is a kind of hell
a kind of bliss
a kind of gray dream.

I don't want to understand myself.
I want to cleave to the casting away
to be held up by the abundance
of how many loves?

Whomever I have loved
love now
I hold to me
escapeabley.

I want to float awhile on this gray brocade gondola
and ask where am I? to no one
and hear the echo
am I? am I?

Going nowhere slow
slow take me slow
we're all alone in this together said the clock to the mouse
and tirra lirra and fiddle dee dee
whose acolyte shall I be?
I choose darkness and calm
I choose the dreamer
will the dreamer choose me?
For I'm under the stars, fast asleep
and I'm counting my blessings
(instead of sheep).

A Merciful Act of Corroboration

All this last year I've wasted time
writing in my journal the persistent question
what is this for?

During that time I could have developed
a malicious talent for origami.
I could have drawn a hundred flawed apples
crumpled them
and placed them in a tall stack, struck a match.

I became so exhausted with the shrieking question.
The signs of the struggle, I can show you these.
Tattered pages, the long hairs that fell in multitudes from my head
and lie at the foot of my velvet chair, beside the table
weaving their way into the carpet
where the vacuum doesn't reach.
I can show you the indentations on my fingers
where I gripped the pen too tightly.
I can show you biscuit crumbs.

I began building a library, filling it with books
books on doubt and this unanswerable coffee-stained question.
You see I was never awake.
The question acted as a sleeping drug
a drought.
Against which I drank cup after cup of coffee.
Became clumsy.

I tried to describe the days
forgettable days
I only wanted to jot down
the uncertain memories of a particular ordinary day
complete in its passing.

I wanted to settle into a moment over and again.
There were times when I was barely alive, and wild with it
I couldn't even write the word, perfection
the word, dream.

Instead of a library I should have built a monument to doubt.
I should have spent all my time carving door frames.
Intricate and myriad.
I should have designed this structure
so that it was all doors and windows
windows without glass, open air.

I tell you my time would have been better spent
writing instructions:
tear this page when you discover it
as a merciful act of corroboration.
I hate for you to see me this way.

Go through doors, sit at windows. Sit.
Come and go at will.
Do not waste time.
Do not waste time.

A Change of Course

Was it only this week we changed course?
Or had it been happening in gradations
for some time now?
Suddenly I am one thousand years old.
New again.

We began in earnest eavesdropping on ghosts
speaking to the dead.

In the basement a skull.
Where do you begin painting a skull?
The teeth.
Don't quote me
when I say in death we are finally happy against our will.

Oh yes, I know, it's strange
thoughts of death have made us, the living, content.

This week we collected a bag of leaves in the river valley
and ironed them between wax paper.
Days later the smell pervades
the stagnant green steam of being hangs.
The corpses are scotch taped to windows
to mock the sun.

And I have just begun to discern the barely audible
the dead speaking to the dead
the dead speaking to the living
and to the ghosts of living souls
those spirits, good and bad, that follow you in absentia and cling.

Some are identifiable.
The spider is always my brother.

The hands that shadow-hold mine when I braid my hair
my father's mother.
The laughing tiger that is the mist in the garden
my mother's father.

Most of the rest are yet invisible or birds.
The geese passing over high, moving away.
The sparrows that come and go.
The raven who sat on the neighbor's roof
and ate a small mouse-brown bird
ripping the feathers off to throw, spiraling, at our feet.

Unimperilled, the deep conversation begins.
Is it my imagination or is the path twisting up
becoming a darker, denser green?

Finally, Anonymity

This is the proper moment to become serene.
And then imagine two scenarios.
One, the rug pulled out from under us.
Will it be sore knees or bruised tail-bone?
Chinese or Persian?
Two, it's all as we expected, hoped for.

Gripping resigned exercises in terror balanced
with idiotic hope, strange faith in the unsubstantiated.

We should see uncertainty as the flat top of a verdant hill
somewhere to stand.
The hill is a maze of unguaranteed paths, downward and out.
But let's not start out.
Let's take a seat
and practice
iridescent scorching restraint.

What would you give up now?
Which dreams
adult ones, childhood ones?
Your face in the mirror?

This is no time to dwell on thoughts of being cherished
on not being cherished.
No time for wanting beauty.
It's all imagination now, or it's all a marvelous delusion.

There never was a hill.
You never had to wind down its intricate seething paths
you could have stayed there.
You could have pretended you had nowhere to go
you could have gone on endlessly in that maze

constantly been delivered to the top.
You could have cribbed your way through.
You could have been more clever than all that
given up destinations.
You could have finally achieved anonymity, damn you.

Brittle Leaf

This will be the summer I shall remember
for having given up love poems
as a reminder to love.
The summer I watered the narrow lawn too often
and all the plants grew even so
the plants whose names I refused to commit to memory
lest they failed to over-winter.

This was the summer we habitually watched clouds.
After putting our daughter to bed
we took a glass of dry cold wine outside
and looked up from our books at intervals
until the birds stopped singing.

It was the summer I gave myself stomach aches
worried about everything.
The summer people hung paintings on their walls
forgetting to pay for them.
Or the paintings couldn't find themselves a home
a wall on which to confide.

It was the summer I gave up without trying
longing for the land of my childhood
its birch trees, horses, the quiet
and terrible freedom—
terrible in its unrepeatable wonder and mystery.

We both started dreaming of Italy again, that summer,
we'll say.
Dreamt in a sideways manner
agreed not to speak much of it.

It was the summer I planted too much in the garden
too close. One plant threatening to take over the next.

It was the time I made a clean desperate pact with myself
to stop wanting.
To settle down into myself, into this skin.

It was the summer I made elaborate plans
to write a book and sign it Anonymous
and remain so.
Seeing it was impossible
but that it was all the while happening.
My hair grew lighter that summer
and every word I wrote the sun ate
leaving the paper a brittle leaf.

It was the year I gave summer up before it was quite August
and set my sights on winter.
The only time of year I can think about snow
without a stern boredom and dread.

Regimens of Beauty

What, then, did I know of the regimens of beauty?

My greatest feat, greatest grandest failure—
I have stolen everything
and no longer fear being caught.
My confession, after all, was written crossways
in the manner of 18th century letters.

I am never naked.
So many fine jewels adorn me.
They leave faceted indentations that never rub out, lift.
It hurts only somewhat.

When I refute the charges
it will only be because of my shamefully poor memory
my useless clamoring memory.
After torture, maybe I'll confess to my confession.
Sure I will.
It was self-defense, I'll insist.

But who believes what's written in the future tense?

I can't decide to believe that when one door closes
another opens.
They're all swinging.
Who needs the illusion of imprisonment.

My horoscope this morning said
today my high expectations will be dashed.
I'm not afraid to answer the phone
for once
I'm not afraid to begin with nothing.
Tonight before I sleep I'm going to write a screenplay

of pleasant dreams and when they don't conform
I'll yell cut, cut.
I've had it with the constrictions of dreams.
I'm done with beauty.
I'm done with having it all add up
with symmetry
with powdering my nose.

I'd never have been caught if I hadn't tipped them off.
What I could tell you now about ugliness
after all those years entangled in that regimen of sparkle and glints
no, I'm unable.
May I say, though, I learned less about beauty
than about the effects of a strict debate with fear.

Instead

This morning I will live.
I'll skip the writing and live.
Because I know this is a brief mendacious paradise
my summer yard that still feels
the undulation of snow on its back like a phantom limb.
Even by June the green is still an electric charge.

So yes, I will live.
Watering the green into emerald and fumble-praying
for all the plants yet to flower.
The bee's balm, Jacob's ladder, the stubborn azalea.

I'll pray for the burgeoning and not think about
the unwritten or the stories I saw on the news last night
and the dreams I keep having of dust taking so long to settle
and children with dry lips and blood on busy sidewalks
and my daughter's hopscotch after the sprinkler
overshot the grass.

I won't even think about the house full of lilacs
deepest purple beyond royal
vases and vases
where the bees can't get at them
where right now the blooms don't know
they're dead, amputated, glorious
as they take their shallow drinks of tap water
held in delicate vessels close to the table edge.

I won't think about that breath I will have to take
when I come out of this hot summer morning sun
(where the living really is easy)
and walk into the kitchen
the whole house marinating in deep purple.

I already know the perfume isn't even desperate
the way most perfume is
that the perfume is a note you can almost hear
past asking for mercy.

To Avoid Mirrors

How much easier for a beautiful woman
to avoid mirrors?

I know not.
Only my own aged quarrel with them.
I drag one along with me
furrowing a path behind.
I am the mirror's oxen
a pair of me.
Dull cow eye looking
into dull cow eye.
Though it only seems so.
See how it waters
the teeming waves, the sheen—see there.

The mirrors in my dreams
go on cracking and shattering
of this I have no control.
In the morning I wrap my bloodied feet.
What other course is there?

Is it thanks to the enchantment of the glade
or to what, or to whom,
that I have recourse to one poem.
To one poem
I return and return.
When I read it
I fall into various rooms
of the palace of mirrors
and it saves me consistently.
Never once has it let me down.

In the mirrors, anyone, any visitor,
can say,
It is I.

Having written this—
the secret of the mirror poem—
will it disappear
or close its doors?
And if so what of the glass chair
I am become so fond of sitting in
and what of my mirror-tiled dancing shoes?
And what of me?
Do I turn to silvered glass?

Waiting

It's bad luck to put certain feelings in words.
Who isn't waiting for something?
Isn't that what we're all here for
to learn how to wait?
There's no point and it's bad luck to talk
about being discontent.

Anyone can adopt a tone of despair.
It helps first if you lose your nerve for daily tasks.
That way you can be at a loss
just the state you need to cultivate despair.
I've lost my nerve for cooking.
Soon we'll be living on milk and cereal.

Waiting. Even the word
contains a thousand questions.
Arrivals, departures,
presentiment.
It's a knack
we learn as children and then know it so well
forget we're doing it.
Mostly we wait for one feeling to leave
another to arrive.

It's not so bad.
Many people develop a parlor trick.
Or concoct a story to haul out in company.
There are always knives
or procedures involving silk scarves.
It whiles away the time.

I'm learning to disappear.
Every week I'm a little closer.

My blackened fingertips
drop the empty matchbooks to the floor
with ever more faith.
One day I'll be in flames
turn around
and that's when finally
the door appears.
I'll be ready, I won't hesitate
to walk through.

In Readiness

In readiness
I wrote a love letter to Nothing
lined the envelope with the dampened
moss of my soul.

I've made plans to divest.
But haven't executed them yet
due to a precocious weariness.

My stated goal
is to write the poem
that desires not to be read.

So pure and alone
it gives off no light, no shadows.

Unlike this one
that must end with rainbow Christmas lights
strung all along the last line
flashing in time to that soundless tune
its name on the tip of my tongue.

Doors and Windows

It's best not to remain imperturbable
when you've become deadened.

It doesn't upset me that all these words will go missing
as most words eventually will.
Their disappearance won't change anything.

But even I can't quite believe the perfect book
has no pages.

Whatever fears and desires
I could have given voice to this morning
were superceded by a frightful blankness.
I can't tell you how disquieting.

All the doors are closed.
Only the mind can open them.
They only open when you listen to them singing.
Attention to radiance is the first note.
How did I become deadened?

I made everyone go away
so I could escape.
I'm alone. Listening.
Straining to hear that song, wedge my foot in a burning door.
But all I hear is hammering and sawing
from the house being built behind ours.

The only thing that might free me
from the delicate grinding around my eyes
is that I can fill this page up without even
the magic words
and yet have faith they will disappear

all to the tune of hammer and saw
hammer and saw.
That someone will have jumped through
the gawking open doors and windows
even if it wasn't me.

Dragon, Tiger, Lion

For some painters, a face
for others a mountain, a certain faceted landscape
oranges, a lion.
The same goes for writers
the compelling theme.
You choose it, it chooses you, doesn't matter which.

I had mine narrowed down
to—inhalation or exhalation.
But after thirty-six years I've forgotten how to breathe.

The newspaper goes on printing pictures of people
jumping out of a collapsing building.
I hold my breath for them, that they may still take wing
that the wings may not be waxen.
When someone goes through a red light
I hold my breath
don't want to get broad-sided again.
When my daughter goes off to play at the house on the next block
I hold my breath tight
her feet so small, so small, pounding hard on the cement.

These mornings of mine, alone, I stop altogether.
That's when I begin my study of clouds.
What else can be done?
Dragon, tiger, lion exhalations.
But today it is clear
giant cerulean inhalation.
Lungs filling, filling.
Infinity on the uptake.

The Secret Apprenticeship

I'm the art forger again.
As always.
She never leaves me.
That malaise.

I'm apprenticed to her and she is
apprenticed to the dream
within the silence of paintings
to failure.
One comes back to failure
more readily than to whatsoever stands alone.

It has always been my dream to write a version
of my life and sign it, Anonymous.

Well. Tomorrow I am dead.
I write that everyday in my diary
so I will have written one true thing.
But no. Don't believe that.
I'm not even brave enough to do that
it might come true.
All the same
that's why I must hurry
write this letter to you
instructions on
anonymity.

There are no instructions.
And the diary I have been keeping
all this long while
never was mine.

The great masterpiece never had about it
any paint.

The Masterpiece

Where are You?
I woke up asking that to the ceiling.

Is this blasphemous,
I don't believe that god should be capitalized.
It's not necessary.

I know this much.
The masterpiece is unsigned.

The Technique of Foreshadowing

It's good that we've fallen to pieces.
No, we don't know what it is to fall.
No we've no idea what it feels like to be broken.
Sure we've stepped on the shards of ourselves
once every blue moon.
Dug them out with clean pocket knives.

Once I made a whistle with a red knife.
An adult knife, and I was a child.
They don't give knives to children so often these days.

I spent hours looking for the right sapling to sacrifice.
Stripped away bark, scraped the green juice.
Smoothed, hollowed the yellow-white bone.

I can't believe it even now.
That it worked
that it made a sound.
I don't remember the sound
only that it made one.
Why didn't I keep it?
I didn't keep it.

I know I'm only imagining I buried it
by that fallen tree near the slough.
It's ridiculous to attempt to speak about the magical places of childhood
the moss and spider webs, unearthed tree roots, birch bark.

Did I think this would yield a tree that would whistle
windless
and I could hear it from any future?

I was careful.
Didn't so much as knick myself with that knife.
Don't know why now I feel that as a lack.
Have always had a distrust of the technique of foreshadowing.
Always I'm listening
and there's not even silence
not even that.

Cream

Finally, it's merely the shocking embarrassment
of finding oneself alone.

Do me a favor
don't read anything into this statement.
That's how it is in periods of misery
however short-lived, however stark.

Emotions handsomely felt.
Savored even.
Don't hold them against me.
I try and keep them true
these weak utterances of despair.

What's to be done when you were meant
to examine darkness
but are continually cursed with flowers?
Hard blessings everywhere
strewn like petals.

I even betray myself—
my black bitter heart—
by pouring cream in my coffee.

An Instant

Everything's going to be fine.
Really fine.
How many times have I said that and only hoped
I believed it, this urgent and remote placation.

I know it
this instant.

It's mine, this thought.
It's cupped in my hands.
Like fresh fallen snow.
And I'm not staying here with it, in the warmth of this room
I'm walking out the door
leaving tracks in the sticky snow
going to sit on the bench by the leafless lilac trees.

I'm going to watch my breath awhile.
Let my eyelashes turn into fluttering icicles.

My toes are going numb.
There's a white spot on my cheeks.
I'm going to forget my name.
Start talking crazy.
I think I'm turning into garden statuary.

Will I be covered in moss by spring?

Deep summer, I'll come back in.

Everything will be fine.
You'll see.
Fine.

Skinned

It happens so easily. I should be glad.
That I have the aptitude.

The simplest things break my heart now.

At breakfast
the heft of shells skinned from the boiled eggs.
The gray kitten staring out the window at falling snow.
Words crossed out in a letter
so that even the dots and loops and crosses are blotted.
In the evening
I am untouched by the sun's
bleeding face scraping down the horizon.
And in the darkness I wonder how a being
becomes so cold.

My heart breaks easily.
But it never dithers.
It jumps back to the queue
hoping to volunteer as witness for the lesser
of whatever heartbreaks are to be handed out that day.

Lost Heart

I should go looking.
In thick forests
the metropolis
elsewhere.
I should pin up signs in dark tunnels.

When it's ready it might return.

Perhaps with the heaped snow
on the front stoop
I'll set out a saucer of milk.
Or the axe.

The Chant of a Small Existence

If I have lately betrayed happiness
it has been an honest betrayal.

I've suddenly begun to hear it—
the chant of a small existence
and I can't get it out of my head.

Mornings, the dream taste is altered.
The taste of melancholy has altered.

There is an odd sadness that accompanies one
when one begins to notice, really notice
the way things begin to repeat and repeat.
The inner climate, the inner terrain.
Which before had seemed to have a forward movement
and a backward movement
now seems constantly sidelong.

The resistance to settling down into a life—
this induces sadness as well.
Knowing that so much more will be known,
revealed,
from here on in.

Please know, this is not complaint.
For I have complained too often
which has drowned out the possibility of joy.

Sadness, I believe, is embraceable.
There is a solemn and blessed freedom in melancholy.

Falter

It's not enough to say, regrettably
that faltering is cowardice.
Only a coward says regrettably.

I had been vanquished by winter
the endlessness of snow.
I had lost the will to disappear.
It made me fearsome.
And afraid.

Every choice I made seemed fraught.
Instead of clutching them to me
they began to drop
like articles of clothing
from an armful of laundry.
I was going up stairs tripping
on warm washcloths, dishtowels, socks.
I put them on the bed to sort
when I could have flung them down the stairs
through railings to the basement
to land on the cement.

It's easy to see the whole thing now
as a comedic gesture.

But when you falter
it's a plunge into the brittle chasm.
For a moment you're in the leaking dripping catacombs.
You've come unhinged from your own existence
and it's only a thread that's fished you up again.

Worst, you saw the key
down there on the wet clay bottom
and were too concerned with scrabbling upward out
that you didn't reach down and claw it from the abyss.

Waking into Darkness

Unmoored, this is the time for measuring
kinds of emptiness.

Within the blindness of winter
waking into darkness.

The sun begins to rise
and instead of relief
a renting of the flannelled soul.

If only
the snow would have fallen thick
blocking out the sun this morning.

The collected data, incomplete, is tucked into the sleeve
as a mother stows tissue for her unhappy child
forgets it until her black shirt has gone through the dryer.
The garments, clouded.

At first it seems the emptiness has made the insidious mess.
Touched everything.

That you've witnessed a star-show of deferred sorrow
dawns more slowly
the careful measure of light clinging obstinately
to dark.

An Idiot

I hunt under doors for a glowing
that I hardly ever glimpse.

I am an idiot entertaining
impossible dreams.

Sadly,
she smiles,
most days
I am pleased with that.

Not Once

But twice.

I was emptied, shelled
from a dream into the dead
of last night.

I had no questions.

Was it more like being
rolled into a ditch from a slow moving car?
Or was it like falling out of an apple tree
fruit untasted, hungry, plucked.

These came later.
Then, it was just the scraped out feeling
sitting on my chest purring
its otherworldly breath entering my open mouth.
Knowing
I had to quickly eat
the curdled dream placenta
or sleep would never come for me
nor serenity.

Closely Unremembered Dream

The scent just out of step with me all day.

Has somehow joined itself in my mind
with the mysterious glory of the sun arising
the quiet revealing of the kingdom
this morning
the black shell gently peeling back.

I've had this sort of dream before.
The sort that lingers all through until
once again sleep calls.
You take it into the known caverns
of falling into the deep.
Only when you awake in the morning
has it truly left you
has it become part of the fabric.

Today I have carried around with me
a hazy train station
a nearby café in smudged charcoal
a spring green glass on a small round table, uneven
the glass filled with a syrupy amber-pink
dream-taste.

Halfway into afternoon and I want
to carry it through the day, all through.
I hardly look left or right—
it's like balancing Shakespeare and the Bible
on my head
down a hallway filled with doors.

What of the few, very few dreams
that make it back to the sleep realm?
Are they folded into more dreams until clotted enough
for a world?

This one, written down—its chance must be spoiled
already it has changed.
It floats, yet, but not peripherally
and my tongue, lost,
doesn't know it.

Courier

Maybe the trouble is there is too little
to be bitter about
in the summer's end of this cold climate.
I spend my morning being angry at August
for its pitiful and glorious last blooming.

During which time the skull Rob ordered arrives
delivered by courier
in an uncrushed cardboard box.
Not even the corners are dented.
Inside, the skull is packed in styrofoam.

It's a replica.
Our shivers, false.
We won't be haunted by a spirit
who wants us to take a distant relative to tea
we won't have to buy expensive flowers
to lay on the grave of the deceased's mother.
Our candles may remain unlit.
Our house won't burn down by accident.

Only one died
so that hundreds, maybe thousands,
of replicas could be sent to those
who study endings.

The box says "Skulls Unlimited" on the side.
We can only hope this remains true.
We can only hope the supply is mercifully steady.

Unbidden

And then it arrives.

As though it hadn't been there
all along.
And all along it has.

It arrives on its lovely lion paws
warm and dusty and well-worn.
Unbidden it kneads you open
and tenderly devours your meager heart.
There you are—whole at last, at last
alive.

Love arrives
I'm talking about the grand love of life and oh,
everything.
Love arrives
and it's true it was there
all along.
Do you think it won't leave again?
Do you think it won't leave and return
again and again?

This Joy That Hovers Within

There is this joy that hovers within.
I'm ashamed to say I hardly own it.

All the other flotsam
in this whirlwind of my own making
am I intimate with.

I won't own joy.

But I know that in the early mornings
it moves closer
needing only strong coffee
a long gaze into darkness
one dangling thought
containing no words, no words at all.

Winter is Never Tranquil

I am pleased that winter has come yet again
for I have hated this season
white limbo
and I mean to make amends.

I'm going to ignore the frostbite
and my chapped, flaking skin.
In the morning I'll not turn up the furnace
nor re-heat my coffee when it's past lukewarm.
I'll stop pouring chamomile and lemon juice on my locks.

I'm going to set it straight between us at last.

I'm going to write what I can.
The simplest, lonely things.
I'll invent a script
tall letters with subtle, unaffected flourishes.

My daughter, 4 years old
said to me the other day
why do you look so sad?
I could have cried with joy.
All the fine lines a day holds.
Scribbled into a design that could be
an indecipherable masterpiece.

I'm going to set that down.

Did I say that I planned to write my love of winter
onto the smooth white icing
in the backyard?

My fervent wish is for frequent snowfall.

Oh, but listen.
You and I know winter is never tranquil.
The forecasts hardly ever predict the biting storm.
Still I can dream that I'll tell myself
whatever it is I need, whatever comforts.
Fifty types of comfort.
Until the cold fire in my heart is a white ember.
Slow-burning, warm.

Cabin Fever

Hear me.

I can tell you precisely
why it is unnecessary
to read these words.
These words
these words
of someone learning to become snow.

See this path I take
these constant false premonitions
the unloveliness of this hunger.

Every year is the same
winter arrives and I wander stumbling
and I try to love, limitless
but I am not even a wanderer
always arrive at this cabin.
Pray don't follow.

I arrive by two paths.
On one I believe I am accompanied by the lion of the snow
the other I am running away.

Who in their right mind runs from love?

I'm given everything I want.
Paper, ink, myrtle.
The hush.
I reach the correct temperature.
Pure ice.
You would see right through me.

And all I can do is yearn
for a hand on my rib cage
a chisel, a hammer.
Which is enough for the return to earth.
Or clay, or mere marble.

But what use is it to warn
of the fever that comes when the shattered crystals of the self
rest in front of the cric-crackling fire.
When one is neither firm nor fluid.
When one wants to be both indoors and out.
When one needs equally happiness and sadness.

Snow Dragon

In winter the sun takes too long to come up
and hair takes too long to dry.
Before noon, the squinting blue sky will give you headache
and fingers are always cold.

In winter we know endlessness
but it's too cold to hold in our mouths.

In winter I am filled with a sluggish envy.
An inner white forest brambled with staining red berries
jabbing thorns.

In winter I need new jeans
but I never get them.

In winter there is always something not quite right.
Winter is a baleful excuse.
For which I am both grateful and resentful.

In winter there are no dragons.
But there should be.
Great white scaly things
made of fog and granulated sugar
and a tongue of white fire.
Something to blame all this unrest on.
Something to blame for the lacerations
on the blue naked bodies
of all those who lost their balance.

Red Mouth, Black Stomach

I like to sit, quiet
and look into the future.
I like to think about letters I wrote
long ago
that were never sent
words still traveling in their crumpled boats.

Nowadays, I have no choice
I send everything.
I take the red mouth of the mailbox very seriously
I take the black stomach even more so.

The years swirl around me, the past
in all its tattered finery.
But without trying, I am ever more adept
at fixing my eyes at a point beyond
the sights and deaf sounds of whatever was.

I could turn into a pillar of salt.
But luck keeps a wind scattering me forward.
I always escape.

I confess, I don't send everything.
But now, when I write a letter
I light it on fire
leaving small piles of ashes behind, and salt.

Don't ask me why my fingers are singed black.
Don't ask me about the scent of burning flesh
that lingers in my yellow hair.
Look in my eyes and see
how mirthlessly
longing will mingle with contentedness.

To Prefer the Wistful

I've tried on so many clothes
and have yet to find
the correct silk jacket.
The one with the embroidery I have in my mind.

When I was young on a visit to Hong Kong
I could have bought it.
It wasn't that I knew I would outgrow it.
That it would be worse to have the correct jacket
perfect, in the wrong size.

No one thinks ahead to what shape they will become.
But why couldn't I have bought a swatch of cerise silk.
Why couldn't I have learned to embroider?

It is a bad habit to prefer the wistful glance into time.

I want to learn to embroider
dragons and mythical birds and orange trees.
I want to prefer silk
and forget about the rickety days
when I would have embroidered
every dragon into my pale skin.
It's hard to believe even now
that I walked with sloped shoulders
in the streets of Hong Kong.

In the Night, Dead Night

So you find the way to make your skin
transparent
pounding it like a mollusk
in the dark dead kitchen.
You've learned to drape it
stretched over chairs.

You find a way to remove your heart
through the third and fourth ribs
how to slide it out and place it in the freezer
by the pork chops and loaves
and let it stay while you sleep, dreamless, awhile.
You've learned to wake up before the crepuscular moment
and stab through slush to red ice without breakage.
So it aches and throbs when you replace it, alone.

You know how to bleed into stainless steel bowls
from the inside of your elbows.

You know how to read your own entrails
and then stuff them back in so the next time
they'll tell no secrets.

All this, it's all for naught.
Raw things, whole and broken
may be uttered by anyone
who would open the letter
under the titanium sun in the public square.

And anyway, whatever you would have said
the weak streetlight at midnight
illuminating your washed feet
would have answered.

Let's Not Kill Moonlight, Again

And again.
I arrive at the unsettlement.
How can this be?

I attempted to splice the morning moon, full
into my eye
but it kept avoiding my glance.
That white yawn, cage
of the inward breath, sharp-drawn.

I sit here now, self-conscious
look at the ends of my hair
a recurring fascination/repulsion
with split ends.

I would rather in the final draft
leave myself out.
I would rather hand the moon over
to the proper authorities
than say—
early this morning the moon
swallowed me
when I wasn't looking
into its thirsty eye.
And now I can focus on nothing
of any importance
for that matter or worse
of true insignificance.

The Prevailing Wisdom

Of all the myriad kinds of solitude
the one I love best
that old solitude of failure.
The kind that begins in one direction and ends up
half-lost, in another.

The prevailing wisdom
is that you should leave out the imperfect.
If I turned imperfections into puffs of smoke—
what a lot of smoke.
If the smoke stayed, thick and banded
with imagined colours
then maybe I'd agree.
But it always thins and rises and leaks out the windows.

Even though I saunter
I'm in a terrible race.
Not knowing where I'm going
means there's no time to lose.

I'm ardently impatient.
I give myself to the poem
it doesn't want me.
Here I am again.
I'm not enough.
No one is.

At least I'm persistently fickle in my lovesickness.

I used to think that it wasn't enough
to merely become pure as ice.
That I'd have to be as carved and shaped
as a sculpture on a banquet table.

An elaborate ice-phoenix or sea queen.
Now I'd give anything to be unformed
glistening, gleaming, melting
perishing, unnoticed, under the spotlights.

The Opposite Will Occur

After a period of contentment
the opposite will occur
all things being more or less equal
and no one knows why.
It must be one of the grandiose mysteries.

But instead of trying to suss it out
I sit and imagine
the end of the world.

It's a human predilection to imagine the end
with as much drama as possible.

But the picture I conjure, lackadaisical, isn't flames
reaching recklessly for the sun.
I don't imagine floods, famine, or freezing.
For me it's the beginning again.
Only this time scratch the humans,
add birds.

Every tree would be equal to the weight of birds
feathers would collect in dips and valleys.
Gravity would be lightly tested.
The sky would be constantly jeweled by flight.
Always the dazzling balance
between aloft and alighted.

Wreathed in Gray Flowers

I won't know for a few years
but I think I disappeared this morning
I peered into the brink
and returned.

What I mean by this
is one of the indelible scenes of an existence
was created.

You don't need a photograph to remind you—
a photograph would kill it.
Those moments that have nothing in common
with movies, with film.

Our minds store them up for dying.
My theory is you fall backward
into the accumulation of magic and joy
those moments where your body disappears
when you aren't looking at yourself looking
when you break up into infinitesimal particles.

Dying, I'm falling back into a tangle of pea-vine
birch trees, moss, the birch clearing
I'm holding wild strawberries, small jewels, in my cupped hands.
I'm in the middle of ten horses.
There's the night on the dark spruce road
there's my friend with the long red tresses
in the ditch there did we both see Jesus
truly and with awe.
Then late, in the sculptor's backyard
I meet love, in the moonlight and rubble.
We turn a corner, the forum in Rome.
Our daughter born, her eyes, her eyes.

And then once at the beginning of spring
I fell into the gray horizon full of snow
I looked out the window
and died
and when I returned
I was robed in gray flowers
my hair wreathed in gray flowers
and I knew to write this all down
exactly as it is.

The Blue Feast

Sometimes a city, sometimes a clearing
or a veranda hanging under the plain miracle of sky.
I want to escape.

It's better to sit
after all the interruptions
and drink silence
or whatever resembles silence.

I think draped thoughts about those moments
of limitlessness
where you see your life could be anything
that there are a thousand eyes in each moment.
After, I reach my hand to the shelf
and open a book and there it is.
How can this happen so often?

How is it that every animal
that has entered my heart
has always had a small white diamond on its chest—
Arabian horse, black lab, blue tabby.

Our honeymoon on Sardegna.
The blonde lab that followed us for a week
so that she seemed to own us.
Up the long paved road from the grocery store
to the villa with the red tiles
and the rosebush by the stone bench
where I read Italo Calvino while
the ants crossed my feet.
I knew this dog who watched over us
this dog with the white kiss on its chest.

I want to escape, it's true.
But I've no need to travel.
I want to escape into, not from.

It's enough to sit and remember
the smallest markings, repeating.
It's enough to fix my eyes on the horizon
as though standing on that stone bench which overlooked the sea
filling myself on the blue feast.
It's enough to feel again
the stabs of recognition—
how fetterless they are.

The Clearing
✳ ✳ ✳

Thoughts for a Slight Poem

On the scene of watching
husband and daughter drive away.
Waving, blowing kisses.
I always forget to catch them.

Because I have seen the next scene
on tv or read it in the paper
every time it is death.
I'm busy killing them in my mind
in that huge intake of breath and rebuke.
I swallow them
lose them to the air.

There they go.
Good-bye.
See how easily I entrust them
to ten year old metal and uncertain mechanisms.
I entrust them to pitted roads and
I entrust them to other blurry people in huge cars
who forgot to go for an eye examination.

It's too sentimental
this slight poem
where I kill them.
The whole time I'm thinking about it
ashes, ashes.

Soon, they'll be home safe
roses in their cheeks.
They've missed me, if only a little.

And here I am licking my black thin lips with wild remorse
not even having choked once on all these words in rows and lines.
Here I am
having traveled with lions.

Angles

Yes. That you are shattered
when you have a child.
And every birthday each
shattered piece of you
shatters again.

When she comes running
every step.
When we are apart, with every fathom.
When she gets out a bowl,
some cereal, milk.

The light enters sharp
through so many angles
when you have a child.
It is as though
you are constantly raised
above ground and let go.
The hard earth you begin to know intimately.
Such exhaustion and joy.

The Last Word is Always Wrong

Before, when I imagined my death
I was exultant.
I didn't believe it.
But now, a mother, the flowers
burst into flames.
You can't snuff them out like candle flames.
The nerves in my fingertips are hereafter condemned.

Now when I kill myself
the last word on my lips,
No.

It should be, love.
Love.
But the last word is always wrong.

It's morbid, I can't stop trying to write a poem, then.
Something like the last poem.
It contains the proper message.
And is addressed to the one who is motherless.

Any advice would be wasted.
Children don't need advice
they need love.
But you can't fill a box
wrap it with pink tissue paper and tie it with ribbon.
You can't send it
it never arrives.
Can't save it.

She screams in a tired-out rage.
I nod my head.
She falls into dreams

my fingers trail down her small soft back.
I laugh at her song and dance.
Every gesture love love love.

Look at her.
How beautiful she is. I know her laugh by heart.
When she is thirty
I want to sit by the now spindly apple tree in the backyard
and tell her how she changed me.
How love printed itself on my cells
erasing the last word.

Clearing

A particular clearing hovers
at the back of everything I am.
There it is at the back of every attempt
every failure.
They're all failures, I know.

Here, can I find a place for it here?
I keep asking
but it has no home
always just on the other side of the door.

The clearing repeats
as a great core of silence.

Did you know this?
How few secrets we have.
I hardly remember it.
On the way there
(I could only find it twice
only when I wasn't looking for it)
on the way there
a birch tree struck by lightning
fungus growing on the side.
I hardly remember it
the sun throbbing through the leaves
like a thousand angels blinking
calmly shocking the back of my eyes.

I keep trying to return
to this place
where lessons are given
on flame
on falling upwards.

But that is not all.
The secret is, don't tell, don't tell
the secret is I am trying
to become that clearing.

No, the real secret is the fear
that my daughter won't have this
and it is my fault.
I weep for her every lost joy.
The secret is
it's my fault.

Arrow in the Calf

I can't empty myself.

The mother-worry deep and violent as orchids.
Just the everyday worry mothers will have.
Just that.

Yesterday walking in the Japanese garden
it's revealed that certain things wouldn't come to me
this time, in this life.
A jeweled quiet, for one.
And a few others. It's not important to talk about.
I could stop longing for them.
There's no point being inconsolable.
That was that.
An understanding like an arrow in the calf
so painful it's painless, accepted.

Today I can't feel the arrow.
Still, I can't empty myself.

I can't stop thinking about one afternoon this week.
The green yard filled with steamy children in bathing suits
nymph-damp hair
learning to get along.
One found a thistle in the grass.
How offended she was.
And I, I felt guilty, and yes
angry.

At the thistle at the child
that the thistle belonged to me.
I was angry on behalf of her bare feet
on behalf of mine.

Why was I responsible for this thorny weed
that had risen unbeknownst to me
on my grass so green no one would know it was a drought.

Why is every sharp message delivered with pain.

How is it ever possible to be clear? How?

The Calm is a Drape

It's idiotic to feel bliss
when all you have to do is turn on the television
to see the dead.

The day goes by and I hardly think of ugliness.
There's an explanation for most things.
The worst is waiting for some money to come in
to pay the bills.
I wish the news would go away
I'm that selfish.
I'm tired of dreaming of limbs too far away from bodies.
And I'm tired of waking up thinking
it would be idiotic
not to feel bliss.
I don't want the thinking, just the bliss.
The coffee tastes so good white with milk
and the lemon poppy seed cake.
The sky is clear, azure, and in the early morning
the calm is a drape hanging before heart's window.

Then my daughter awakes and comes to where I'm reading poetry.
Sits on my lap warm and heavy with dreams
her head on my chest
my cheek on her curls.
When she moves
I want to hold her back but I don't
I help her down, gently, impossibly.
She lands like a cloud bird,
changes into a girl and runs from me.

I keep these moments, store them up.
Don't even know what for.
Against what.

Commonplace Secrets

I forgive you.
Keepers of my forgotten secrets.
But no.
I almost forgive.

All my scattered confessionals
I remember you
lavender apparitions
and how I said words
into your throats and eyes
that even I have forgotten.
Almost forgotten.

Each day I wake up soft
a new person
and by nightfall I've hardened into
what I've always been.

The most difficult thing to say
at any given moment
need not be horrific.
But merely the commonplace
that has been hidden
by fierce habit, buried shame
or the daily fear of existing.

When I dust against such secrets
I am startled
but only in that sidelong way.

Past Infatuations

Those accidents of loneliness
one comes back to
like the photograph that keeps falling from the book
coming unglued
and you stoop to pick it up
shocked to see it out of time, out of context.

The object of infatuation doesn't matter
has become banal, sits on a chair and smiles
at something in the distance not you.
The object of infatuation is just that
and can be remembered with a commonplace tranquility.

Not so the feeling. Not so.
Can't be given away
attached to my skin like a permanent
deeply layered sunburn
light and crisp as French pastry.
I must still be in love with a magnificent abandonment.

No. I don't know what these past feelings come to mean.
Except they are what love is not.

But there they are, these old used hearts
everyone has a couple
hanging to dry
refused Valentine cards.
An image so saccharine it must be true
perfectly fitting to the non-occasion.
Trying to remember how the heart remembers.

Of course they're blowing in the wind
the finishing touch
they come unpinned
rise the way paper blackened from a bonfire rises
with a charming darkness.

I have them to thank for the spots in my soul
burns from a cigarette
and for my penchant for pretty self-torture.
And though I yet have an insatiable desire for happy endings
when I sit down to write the dry story of my existence
I know it will inevitably be bittersweet
but that I will stop the pen before it reaches a melodramatic tragedy.

Trains and Apples

No one thinks they'll ever need what they fail
to learn in math class.
They should teach the secret mathematical equations
that make up a life.
In a happy marriage for example.
The bad given up for the good
or the good taken away and the bad made unknown.
They should teach the delicate incriminating calculations
made for love in dreams and back-alleys.

They should abandon problems with trains and apples
and try and resolve why one person
will be born in love with the world and another
will be born choking on love.
How one who was meant to be a piano prodigy
ends up a typist.

And departures.
What forces take some people away
and leave others stationary?
Please explain the relationship of distance to the heart.

When our friends leave now after the holidays
it's just one big sigh and a shrug.
Refusal and resignation all knotted up
tucked into the closet
with the bows and nearly empty rolls of wrapping paper.
I admit feeling anger at what separates us.
Nothing so easy as distance.
The worst is that dull ache
the way you must pretend it isn't there.
What's the point in entertaining dullness?
Having it in for tea and cake only exacerbates.

Too intimate.
Best to meet in a café and beg off early.

In math class they should at least teach
how to erase the chalk from the board
how to keep it from leaving marks
on the front of pants.

"In Our Next Lives as Horses"
(for B.L.)

I want to talk about the way a life enters a life
cause and effect
the way our particular paths have crisscrossed.
The singularity and the sameness and the necessity.

I believe in existence as both forest and clearing.
I believe, as you wrote,
in our next lives as horses
this tethered, tarrying sojourn
where we, groping, plunge
into the illuminating darkness, worlds within worlds.

In one, we are Chagallian—
red velvet and blue lace skyhorses.
Though when I say lace, you should know I do mean grace.

In another, we straddle clearing and forest.
I can feel the full force of that next life, here.
I can lean into it
as a horse, long-haired, flowing and unhaltered
leans on a tree in winter—
not merely to rub the dry itch or soothe the cold ache
but as a rich comfort.
A reassurance
that in the white season
still the roots hold
there is yet a little sway
and yet firmness.

The Dead

The dead always visit me
in the form of large speckled
spiders.
I wish they wouldn't.

Yesterday there was one on the fence
hovering in its perfect web
over the bee balm
scarlet lion's tails.
I had meant to show it to my daughter
my fearless beloved.
Today it's gone.
Even spiders move on.
I am left to read the sky
and once again
ponder those things I never quite got right.

By now it's such a tired subject I don't have lift off.
Don't reach sorrow.
These days I realize the web is the message
and not the spider.

These days I look at the clouds.
The sky has given me a long line
ethereal handwriting
that feathers its way into a creature
made entirely of spines and ribs.
Yes, I look at the clouds alright
but I do know
I know this at last
that the message is sky.

The Various Tricks of the Dead

Wasn't there a rule
that in winter
there shan't be any
visitations?

I thought this and in the dark early calm
one morning
was proved wrong.

The photograph of my grandmother—
my grandmother who became anonymous
after giving me my father—
the photograph in which I always search
and see
my own face, my own eyes
came alive
with my brother.

Such are the various tricks of the dead.
He's left since.

But I am still reminded
of how we fail the dead
how the dead fail us.

The dead appear to sew messages
into our eyes
that we are condemned to decipher, blind.
This time was it
to love?
To melt down guilt and confusion
to melt down what can't be understood
turn it into love.

The dead must feed on love
and I have been hoarding it
here in my earthly room.
One shouldn't blame them
for arriving like wet cats at the back door
early mornings
to cry their dark calm hunger.

When We Meet Again After Being Apart for a Year

A year of questions and answers in letters.
Some answered some not.
Time still for the questions we didn't know to ask
over wine and steamed mussels
while the snow falls on our cars.
We'll have changed, yes.
My hair will be longer, but it's already long.
You see I still don't care about it
I'm still vain about not caring.
The changes won't matter.

I sent you a photograph of dandelions
stuffed into a plastic blue cup
you answered with one
of a toad in a mayonnaise jar.

How grand a friendship like ours
how enviable.
I stand back and am jealous myself.

Letter to A——, June 14

Of course the contentment never lasts.
What would we do with it anyway?
The sky blue every morning
we'd run out of words to describe it.
Azure, cerulean, sapphire.

We'd hear all the robins and chickadees
the gentle breeze rattling the soft leaves
of new trees whose blossoms lie around them
like a funeral wreath on the grass.

But we'd neglect all those noises
that lead to headaches
that enter at the base of the neck
invisible serpents squeezing and licking
with electric knife tongues into our thoughts.

Content, we'd forget to wonder
if we were understood.
By someone, anyone.
It wouldn't matter in our contentment.
Whoever would look at us there on the patio
in the sunshine holding a cold perspiring drink
would know us to be unconcerned
with esoteric knowledge.

Next time we're together
let's sit in a dark café
and invent new words
and inscribe them into an ordinary coiled notebook
words to describe the colour of the heavens
that blue of a summer morning
one like this.

Unfinished Letter

And I began a letter this morning to you
it said, let's feel every joy.
The rest, the page, is empty.
For once I'm taking my own advice.

If the muse doesn't visit today
I won't turn into sand.
For I am in the kingdom of heaven
the green palace.

But joy is strictly incidental.

I write to you from the backyard.
It's important to say in which seat in the theatre
you're sitting while watching the movie, right?
The blue poppy I keep telling everyone about
there it is out the corner of my mottled green eye
cupping origins, yellow center.

The usual suspects
piled up around me in the form of poetry books.
The wind keeps catching at their pages
and I attempt to heed which poem ruffles to the top.
I'm satisfied with the thoughts of others
at least I'm too proud to steal from them
awkward thief.
Tomorrow I won't be so proud.

I don't mind.
Having someone else's poetry course through me
leaving me scraped out and raw.
At least the wound is not entirely mine.
I manage to keep a serene look on my face

getting pink from the sun
the sun that is eating away at the blue poppy.

That dialogue.
I'm eavesdropping.
The sun is saying open relinquish take.
And the response
wait wait
the message.
The blue door.
Joy.
Wait.

What is the gift?

Next. Watering the new apple tree.
Waiting for the muse not to come.
I raise my eyes to the other blue
a lion.
A lion in the clouds.
A lion of the clouds.
Cloud lion.

You can't make something up as simple
as a lion made of cloud
whose lips were pursed
mane flowing backwards and back and away.
What was the form he was kissing?
I strained to see, was I too late, had it dreamt itself
into blue
or was it that I could not fathom
was it a test, or was I too late, or was it a kiss at all?

Gone.

I sat back down.
And began to contemplate the land on the other side
of the fence.
As it happens so often
on the edges of places,
cities
sand, dry dust, sand
I know not how deep.

Truly joy is incidental.

Sunsets and Happy Endings

All my friends leave town one by one.
I've stopped wondering who is next.
I've given up making new ones as I don't want them.
I fill my diary
mainly recording the boiling of pasta
the single glass of table wine taken on an empty stomach.
And then the endless questions
heartbreaking in volume.
Plots on how to reach an honest poem.
Descriptions of flowers dying in unusual vases.

January is a lonely month.
Letters, craved and coveted
are not the friends themselves.
I write back a version of myself
possibly a swankier version
I hope they like it.
I'm glad I'm alone
as alone as anyone.
The first glimpse induces
a blasé shivering.
I should hate to be seen
watching the impossibly early sunset
the sentimental visible in my eyes
the wine burning my heart doubling the scene's glory.

If those who slighted me could see me now.
I wouldn't care.
I forgive almost everyone.
I see the impossibility of throwing oneself into the abyss.

I must be looking at the pink and orange striations
with that
hideous archaic crazy smile
I sometimes cannot help.

Then I drift into melting thoughts of happy endings.
Why shouldn't I.
I know that this very real happiness
comes without encouragement of any sort
is both sweet and fragrant like dessert in the oven
even more painful than despair.

Daring Instruction

※ ※ ※

Daring Instruction

That there are too few metaphors for marriage
or that I'd heard too few.
And that mine was right before me
that marriage is a still life.

I awoke to this thought and it seemed daring
but why I could not yet muddle toward.

There are the constant imperceptible adjustments
to get the composition just so
then waiting for the light
to illuminate the bric-a-brac that means nothing much
to deepen the shadows on the underbellies
of apples and whatnot.
Then something must be taken away
for use in the kitchen
or a child races headlong into the room
and upsets the balance
a wine glass tips over and the rug is bathed in red
the lilies have dropped too many petals
the vase is cracked, damaged
though not beyond repair.
And this replaced with that and the other
until now the colours are all off.
It must begin again.

But once it was perfect and can be again so.
It had been serene and full of tension at once.
There was a mischief about the scene
a hint of uncomposure.

Now in a jumble one sees only the mundane
certainly the unmagical.

The eyes are lost in the moth-eaten pavilion of dailiness.
The rapture of the mundane is that it is unsuspected
that it is itself
mundane.
One turns to it and turns.
Nothing.
Nothing.

And there it is.
The sturdy table is seen again.
One takes particular note of the way
things have a knack for settling in
hunkering down with a difficult poise.
How that alone
is instruction.

The silence of the objects
which speaks to the center of the whole set-up
carries the center off the table, carries it through.

Here I come to the bleakness
the constant scene of dying
here I come to the daring part
which I see now is not daring at all
and anyone in such a marriage will find herself smiling
at the thought of the blemishes and broken stems
at the thought of this perishing feast
for the starved
which does in the end
miraculously
sustain.

Candor

Flirt with candor
research your heart
but do not
utter what does not elude.

What can one say about a marriage
when one is in it
that would not alter its course?
That could be at once true
to the marriage
and true to the self?

Tenderness

Recall beginnings, the lion perfume
that changed your chemical make-up
but do not
obedient, crave nostalgia's too-pretty torment.

Call upon the start instead
as an infusion of tenderness.
Summon it as leaves
summon the thin drag of sap
up the staircase to their green boudoir
disciplined not to romance former incarnations
former unembellished paths.

Refuse to desire anything that has been written.
Fail at anything but tenderness.

Unromantic Aspects

Marriage is not quite a game
of baroque tolerance
but neither is it possible to marry Cary Grant.

You cherish the unromantic aspects
the ticks, the habits, the quirks
but not overwhelmingly.
Though they're sometimes easier to speak of fondly.

Marriage is a book and you discover
you'd earlier on underlined the wrong passages
written silly things in the margins.
The book is still as loved
but the lines you love now are mostly different.
Then it was moonlight on skin and catalogues of flame
whatever was spontaneous
and now
gestures, fleeting knowing expressions
landscape
intellects colliding through time.

A Grumble and a Thump*

If your husband laughs at being likened
to a grumble and a thump
keep him.

If the reader didn't wholeheartedly believe
that Mr. Darcy would learn
to be laught at
the novel would be greatly reduced in popularity
mark my words.

> *Husband. A repressive word, that, when you come to think of it, is
> compounded of a grumble and a thump. (Dorothy Sayers)

Tolstoy*

Unhappiness, if various, is easily defined.
A happy marriage writes
its own dictionary.
Where words like
pain, beholden, resemblance
heartbroken
have lavish meanings.

In a happy marriage, for example
it is understood that sadness
has no propinquity to unhappiness.

An entire book could be written about this.

*All happy families resemble one another, each unhappy family is unhappy in its own way. (Tolstoy)

Hilarity

Some days not so many grand laughs
as they say in the movies
as there are
dry incongruous observations.
Suits me fine.

But it's not without hilarity by any means, fidelity.
This lived movie called
Improvisation on a Dream.

Just yesterday
we cried until
we laughed.

No really, it was funny.
I could have sworn we were a portrait of
Cary Grant and Grace Kelly
hinged to the Arnolfini wedding portrait.

Oranges on the window sill
beside a picnic basket and fried chicken legs.
The dog barking like anything.

Regret

Nothing?

Some days I have no longing.
I only want to sit and be quiet
I don't even want to read
the nectared stack of poetry books I always read
that remind me of everything
I don't know.
I regret possessing this interminable languor.

I regret that when I met you
I didn't instantly take your hand
and run without belongings to Rome
so we could have fallen in love in two languages.

But this is nothing.

I should have mastered the love poem
I should have written a thousand
and begun again
before the love poem became so complicated
unadorned, see-through.

I regret
everything it's too late to learn
everything just beyond my tongueless slipshod grasp.

The Unsaid

Can be a patient friend.

In an insomniac dream
willing myself to sleep
I began to imagine categories
frail domiciles, sanctuaries
for the unsaid.

Not quite words
shapes, my longings
had taken up residence by the sea.
Regard, regard, was what they breathed.
Their house was a glass conch.

My face disappeared.
I had expected to hear, forget, forget.

There is no purification without mindful decorum.

Delicate Somnolents

Many days we live in the fat shrug of exhaustion
we live in the lost and found.
We are oh so delicate somnolents.

Years from now we'll wonder
how we spoke in that waking dream language
how we managed to hold onto the mute threads
of each other.

This looking back from a future I can't yet see—
some would say is uncareful.
I only implore fate to imagine what I will.
That our shoes will be in the same jumble in the hall closet
common annunciations.
That our marriage will resemble
Van Gogh's mud-caked boots.
And that we won't knock them off or scrape them.

I'd like to remember that wet and mucky, tired walk
better than all the others.
The way one day is an embarrassing poem of
not quite unhappiness but something aping it too well
and also how the others are deepened by it.

Let's remember, love,
the flowers you painted over
the leaves you changed into sky
and the words you read aloud to me
and I later crossed out of my poems.
And let's believe, too, in the lost heaven of pentimento
where these bits and fragments
may mingle in a tranquil theory of tapestry.

How To

You can make divining rods
from coat hangers
coat hangers
from divining rods.
The coat
is another matter.

I can't read enough
about mystic friendships
letters between sisters, soul-mates.
I devour the news of Charlotte Bronte's
hunger for letters.
I meditate on the circumstances
of Shams of Tabriz disappearing
from Rumi's back door.
The electric forces of separation—
Rochester calling to Jane—
are a tonic to me.

The desire to be known, fathomed, probed
fades in me
and rises up at once.
A river, in the end
you're known by streams
in ways you can't know yourself.

I can't work myself out to myself.

But I believe in the geomancy of the soul
inner landscapes connecting to inner landscapes
the world of the souls.

Some days I feel my arms are coat hangers
twisted into shape and pulling me
to the dragon current.
It's easy to pour myself into the space between friends.
Others, I feel abandoned to the silent winter winds.

This is when I am most overwhelmed by the generosity
of the coat
that lies bunched up on the floor of the closet
and takes me into its well-tailored embrace
always a perfect fit.

Nice Work If You Can Get It

The work of it—that's plain.
The maintenance of the invisible contraption
the whorl and drone and dross of try try try.
You're given to understand it's a sewing machine
that never quite finishes the alterations
on our best suits, our best selves
but then the machine transmogrifies, discrete
its purpose now ambiguous
now fathomable
now something that flies only on paper
relies on crazy glue and feathers
from mythical birds.
You give it a chance
redesign
re-attune
to the difficult compounding music of the unseen
mechanisms.

You come to understand that the invisible machine
is a device
whatever unusual profiles, particulars
you have memorized
you have created.

What you cannot explain is the tiny mountain
of worn-out stainless steel parts
thin and inhumanly lovely
you have carefully stored in the kitchen cupboards.
The feeling that without them
you would have been deceived
about the accumulation of fine dust, residue
about the encrustations of love and the entanglement of two lives.

They Lived

like suitcases in the lost and found
found but still lost.
They lived in a tangle of deliberate composure
they lived balanced in a dangerous institution
balanced between I and we.

Studies have shown that these words
are doomed to oblivion
for which I am intensely relieved.
I praise the gods.

It's the ecstasy of oblivion
that I embrace.
The ecstasy of the unclaimed.

When I speak to you of loneliness
when I refuse the death of the self
the narrative of the next moment's destiny
it's thanks to the love poem.

If it's easy to revel in an insulated despair
and to sorrow before the pool of unanswerable questions
if it's easy to write fading words patiently
that's because
we crossed out happily ever after together
and decided to take our chances
on the shelf with all the abandoned maps.

Illusions

I haven't given them up
my illusions
cloud castles.
I still like the tricks of funhouse mirrors
and I like saccharine movies where everyone
saves everyone else.

I wish I'd kept those love poems I wrote
that no one would publish.
I wish I could remember where the path began
and which threads I held and then dropped.
I wish I knew where I am.

It's lonely this failure
attempts to speak to someone I can't see
just like myself. No one.

And beside this failure
love.

I have been thinking that love is an atelier
full of attempts and discards and rubbings out.
Love I sometimes think ends
and begins again and again
an unbandaged wound
forsaken experiment in bleeding.
Love only seems continuous
but it clots and then opens
until the sensation is muted, hardly felt.

True love is a fatal grace
an uncertain anguish
because there's hardly room for it.

The days hate love and disparage marriage.

I keep writing knowing that in the end
this is a personal exercise.
I'm writing to tangle rather than disentangle.
Because I'd like to tie it all in knots
the twinkling mirrors on the door of the castle
and the papers strewn on the floor of the atelier.

I promised myself that the poem didn't matter
any more than any other illusions.
I told everyone who would listen that writing poems
was about the process, the transformation
of a life through the writing.
But I do cling to the poem
I do cling to love.

Inexactitude

I had once imagined I would live without need.
I thought this had to do with making do
with the warmth of an unfashionable jacket.

I didn't know the game
for three people
a man, a woman, a child
each holding the others' hearts
arms crisscrossed
circling circling.

The great secret crime of love
is that it is insufficient.
That you could play beautiful simple games
and laugh together and dance.
And that you could feel sadness also.

Breathe, I write in my diary
so many days.
Wanting elegance.
Breathe, I write.

The incalculable number of unpursued thoughts
thoughts intruded upon
the lost questions posed to the hideous days
whatever has been given up
I dare not speak it.
But that is a line from another century.
And I do.

I follow the chafing rope up the mountain
of what I thought our lives would mean

only to become acquainted with the peak
of inexactitude.

What you need and what you have to give
are hardly ever in balance.
It's the way destiny unbeknownst
comes up behind when finally you've managed to stand straight
and sticks you behind the knee.
It's not good enough to follow your path
and try to hold life all in your slender trembling arms.
It's right that you drop
to one knee and scurry about with dirty mice fingers
trying to get it all back
doubting it
longing for what you already have.

Alibi

I believe equally and simultaneously in chance and free will.
I believe in nothing so well as contradictions.

I constantly think of that time we were strangers.
When we might have sat in a café and sipped our cappuccinos
at tables across the room
never glancing at each other.

When we did meet there was a series afterwards
of almost, just barely, not quite.
Phones ringing and then not as I rattled the deadbolt
to my decrepit apartment where water
was turning the sweating walls into papier mache.
Then his long trip to Europe
when I received from other men loveless letters
which I later threw into the garbage can whole, unshredded
uncried upon.

Finally after meeting everywhere
it was the bookstore that brought us together.
Who can say I had not willed it so.

And now as a regular personal torture test of darkness
I intermittently dwell on
what if.
What if one of us were to die.
We would be strangers again
to ourselves.

I know I would keep heart
living a clandestine life
from which I would rarely emerge
to shop in murky bookstores

for that book of answers
the one that never anyway mirrors the book of questions.

If fate can be tempted
my alibi
is that whenever I imagined being alone
my heart was a novel with the last pages missing
and the words on my lips—
from here on there will only be disarray.

Palace of Glass and Stone

(an anniversary poem)

Or how about this one.
Marriage is an uncompletable palace
a palace of glass and stone.

I often wonder where longing goes
never believing it could sublimate.
Gathered over time it appears as an elaborate naïve
structure made of dreams and patience.

I'm reminded of the postman in Cheval
who collected rocks on his country route
first in sagging pockets, then in sturdy baskets.
Carried them home to envelop them in his ideal design.

The years may keep their assigned
paper, linen, diamonds, toasters.

Every day let's pick up shards of broken pop bottles
from the gravel
let's kick at rocks half buried in the earth
pry at them with finger tips and heft them in the palms of our hands
on the dust path home.

Let's take these and
whatever we don't have and make them into
a jigsaw palace
a stronghold.

Looking for Pain

I could easily have gone looking for pain, courted strife.
I have a taste for the sorrow of the world and for folly
and the innocent and foul joy of inebriates.

I even like that other me
the one I never became.
I pity her and once in a while I envy her
Though maybe that's a lie, I don't know.
I don't really envy her.

I've wanted to understand a few things.
And then forget.
Start at the beginning with them again.

I took the sober route.
I didn't go to Italy and become fluent in Italian.
That was only a passing dream.
I didn't drink red wine all day
and write a flippant novel in the piazza.

Instead I fell in love, married, had a child.
And when you have a child everyone has a piece of advice for you.
Some of it good, some of it you don't take. Most of it you don't.
Afterward you wish you'd listened to this or that.
People you've never met stop you
pushing your baby proudly down the street.
She's too warm or too cold or the sun is in her eyes.
Her curly hair, her cheeks, her balled up fists
remind everyone of some baby they've held
some beloved child delivered from the red roiling cloud.
I still can't get over all the shining eyes
the love people don't even know what to do with
they give it to strangers.

Well, as I said, I've wanted to understand one or two things.
Such as how you hold the people you're not, effortlessly and
it's as though the one you are is an egg on a spoon.
I've wanted to understand how you make what you can
from what you've been given.
I've wanted to learn how to sift through the days
to keep love from running through my fingers.
I want to understand how to remain sober and awake
attentive, as though looking after a baby
and at the same time drunk, on my knees
how to give it all away
forgetting remembering everything, a thousand times a day.

Fortune Telling

How we constantly plan and contrive and dream.
This year we buy a chaise longue, a house.
That year we have a child, write a book.
In spring plant a weeping tree
and place a large peach stone beside it
like a fruit pit, outsized.

How every little motion forward
is at least a little off
from what we could have imagined
from the fortunes we told for ourselves
believing them.

But that's what a marriage does
throws white pebbles ahead on the path and hopes
the birds don't swallow them for lack
of bread crumbs.

Delving

This thought—
that the more one delves
into the emotions of the domestic sphere
the more shapes are invented, appear.
That moreover a certain sadness begins a life
and leads you to believe it was always
your fast companion.
And maybe it has been
but you should not believe it.

It is possible to invent a broken heart.
It is equally possible to invent bliss.
Folly to imagine one without the other.

To the Ends

After all the others.
It's the one that goes at the end.
It has to.
It's so far behind you have to squint.

It's there.

After so many words
and after so many brushstrokes
after our days of dabs and breaths.
After the floor is swiped at
and the dishes are washed
and covers tucked, curls mussed, a forehead kissed.
It seems like it must be there.
We're too tired to be entirely sure.
We're sure.

There it is
at the end.
Too exhausted to be much other than what it is.
And yet
it's always enough.
Love.

No

That there will no more be a falling
into
love.
Just.
Love.

Which is so different
so very different.
Kind, gentle, cruel and insane macramé of souls.

The whole way forward
there is that touching memory of
falling.
Which no more can be.

Two leaves fall.
Spiral
and land at the foot of the tree.
The wind, ungracious as ever,
sweeps them up and an age passes
while they travel, rattling, in its varying embrace.

If you were asked to trade
the uncertain eddies, the airy labyrinth
for a constant light and delicious falling?

No.

Acknowledgements

I count my lucky stars to have friends who so generously encourage, inspire and support me in this writing life and in that other schtick we just call 'life.' A heartfelt thank you to: Bert Almon, Kimmy Beach, Heather Carnahan, Meli Costopolous, Olga Costopoulos, Lee Elliott, Vickie Gurney, Barbara Langhorst, Michael McCarthy, Iman Mersal, Nicole Nyenhuis, Karen Petrovic, Michael Penny, Karen Press, Monique Tschofen, Dawn Valentine, Annette Schouten Woudstra. Thanks Erv and Doreen Heiman, and Marilyn Lemay. Thanks to Jody, Jeff, and Tarra. All my love and thanks to Rob and to Chloe.

I am indebted and grateful to Doug Barbour for believing in this book and also for all the fine suggestions he made during the editing process. A glowing thank you to NeWest Press! In particular—thanks to Amber Rider and Katherine Hale at the NeWest office, and to Ruth Linka for designing such a gorgeous book.

SHAWNA LEMAY was born and raised in Edmonton, Alberta. Lemay earned a Bachelor of Arts in Honours English, and has just recently completed her Masters in English-both at the University of Alberta. Lemay lives in Edmonton with her husband, Rob Lemay who is a visual artist, and their daughter Chloe. She currently works for the Edmonton Public Library. Other works by Lemay include *Still* (self-published), *Against Paradise* (McClelland & Stewart), and *All the God-Sized Fruit* (McGill-Queen's University Press)—the winning title of the Gerald Lampert and Stephan G. Stephansson awards.